Compassionate
Cooperation

Terry Hoggard

COMPASSIONATE COOPERATION

© Copyright 2025 — Terry Hoggard

All rights reserved. This book is protected under the copyright laws of the United States of America. No part of this publication may be reproduced, stored in a retrieval system, or transmitted in any form or by any means, including electronic, mechanical, photocopying, recording, or otherwise, without the prior written permission of the copyright owner, except by a reviewer who may quote brief passages in a review.

This book may not be copied or reprinted for commercial gain or profit. The use of short quotations is permitted and encouraged.

Unless otherwise indicated, scripture quotations are taken from The Holy Bible, New International Version, copyright © 1973, 1978, 1984 by the International Bible Society. Used by permission.

Scripture quotations marked NASB are taken from the New American Standard Bible, copyright © 1960, 1962, 1963, 1968, 1971, 1972, 1973, 1975, 1977, 1995 by The Lockman Foundation. Used by permission.

Brian Del Turco served as contributing editor for this project, providing editorial guidance, design expertise, and authoring the reflective elements—including key insights, prayers, affirmations, and practical applications—that frame each section. His collaborative partnership helped shape this work into its final form.

ISBN: 978-0-9986821-0-5

For worldwide distribution. Printed in the U.S.A.

Content

Preface
Special Thanks
About Terry
The City of Brussels

Enriching Your Heart 19

Encouraging Relational Exchange 57

Engaging Your Collective Capacity 89

Afterword

Preface

Behind every book is a "big idea" that was uniquely born in the heart of the author. The desire is always the same—to communicate the "big idea" in a way that is convincing and to have the opportunity to open up a new conversation.

This is clearly my intent and I am committed to doing my best to make this a reality!

Here is my "big idea" …

"All of us have to create processes that enable us to bring people together to accomplish a common goal. And the more diverse the group, the more challenging our task becomes. I call my preferred process 'Compassionate Cooperation.' This book is based on some of the principles I used to craft that process."

Being compassionate provides the opportunity for a team, or a commonly focused group, to openly share skills, sharpen trust and serve each other in order to see an important goal or higher good fulfilled.

Cooperation is the designed and desired outcome, but it is not automatic. There are associated realities which also need to be activated and applied. Things like openness in receiving each other, willingness to accept input and an eagerness to find solutions together.

Certainly, the creation of this process was made possible by the contributions of many! My commitment to "compassionate cooperation" has enabled me to learn something from every person who has ever shared life or ministry with me.

Many voices from many nations have made a major impact on all this process has become.

Their influence is seen in all I will propose to you and their input speaks in all I say.

My hope is that all of this will now live in you,

Terry Hoggard

Special Thanks

I am keenly aware that the places I have been, the people I have met and the pathway that God has ordained for me have shaped my life.

I have served as a European missionary for almost 40 years and have been privileged to see the beauty of God's creation in the most classic cities and villages.

I have met the most incredible people who are truly global citizens, walked into the most amazing opportunities, and at the same time have witnessed the majesty of Christ being expressed in the lives of those who longed to be crowned with His glory.

I have been honored to provide pastoral leadership for the congregations in Rome, Italy; Brussels, Belgium; Copenhagen, Denmark; and Malmö, Sweden. These congregations have touched my life, enriched my heart and deepened my passion.

I am thrilled that my wife and daughters have shared every experience with me. So Ruthanne, Kari, and Kristi ... thank you for always being with me and for me.

I am blessed to have a loving, supportive extended family that encouraged me in 1984 to say "Yes" to what I knew was a life calling to missionary service.

A network of friends who faithfully stand with me in prayer moment-by-moment and honor their financial commitment to us month-by-month surrounds me. This covenant of partnership is more powerful and precious than ever before.

I am grateful to have the most amazing friendship and working relationship with Brian Del Turco. Though family ties may link us, we know that it is spiritual destiny that binds us together. He served as contributing editor for this project, providing editorial guidance, design expertise, and authoring the reflective elements—including key insights, prayers, affirmations, and practical applications—that frame each section. His collaborative partnership helped shape this work into its final form.

Thanks to all of you for sharing the journey with me!

About Terry

Terry Hoggard is a seasoned leader, coach, and connector who has dedicated his career to developing strategic initiatives that foster collaboration across diverse communities and organizations.

Currently, Terry serves in several key capacities that reflect his commitment to building global networks of cooperation. He works alongside the Assemblies of God World Missions and Convoy of Hope to develop a comprehensive global compassion network. As the Relational Leader of Global International Church Network (GICN), which he launched in 2011, Terry facilitates connections among international church leaders and communities. He also engages as a coach and consultant for the Fellowship of European International Churches, a network he founded in 2004.

Terry's thirty years as a European missionary shaped his understanding of cross-cultural collaboration and leadership. During this time, he provided pastoral leadership for congregations in Rome, Italy; Brussels, Belgium; and Malmö, Sweden—experiences that profoundly influenced his approach to bringing diverse groups together around common goals.

He holds a BA in Bible from Evangel University and has completed Master's-level studies in Leadership and Ministry at the Assemblies of God Theological Seminary. Terry is a Certified Life Coach with Coach Training Alliance and a Behavioral Life Coach with the Institute for Motivational Living.

Terry's personal mission reflects the heart of his leadership philosophy: "Love God, cherish my family, value my friends, enjoy people, and aspire to work together with others to encourage them in life and leadership development."

He and his wife Ruthanne have two daughters, Kari and Kristi, who share their passion for ministry and service.

Brussels ... a Place of Desire and Development

Ruthanne and I first saw Brussels together in October, 1995. I visited the city several times in the 1980's, and in 1994 I came again to speak at Brussels Christian Center for their mission convention.

Little did I know this simple invitation would step-by-step lead us to another invitation one year later ... this one to become their lead pastor.

From the very beginning, our hearts were drawn to Brussels — both for the splendid beauty of the city/nation and for the spiritual brokenness we felt so strongly.

What we experienced during our time at Christian Center was clearly divine and supernatural. Our hearts were made one with the congregation, and together we invited the presence of Christ to dwell among us. In response to that desire, God visited us. What He did in, thru and among us was life-changing at every level.

Kari and Kristi both came to Brussels to serve in other ministries in the city, and looking back, we can see their time in Brussels shaped their lives in profound ways as well.

Brussels remains the center of our spiritual activity. Every networking connection I have links back to this wonderful city.

Somehow, deep down, I know what has been birthed in my heart for Brussels was not for a season ... but for a lifetime.

Brussels. My city of "desire and development." —Terry Hoggard

ENRICHING YOUR HEART

"Compassionate Cooperation"... A process that begins with enriching your heart, thus encouraging relational exchange and engaging your collective capacity.

Everything flows from the core. The leader's internal state is the channel of life and wisdom. Internals create and shape externals. What's happening in the relational and external world of the leader can be traced back to their internal world. This dynamic is entirely consistent. The opportunity is that we can steward our internals in a Christ-glorifying way … a way which understands the Kingdom of God and how things truly work. Keep watch over your heart. Start there.

POSSIBILITY
You have to see
   it to redeem it.

Great moments are created as we develop the capacity to see and redeem possibility. This is one of the most important disciplines for us to develop.

The fact is, the possibility does not present itself as powerfully as an opportunity.

Typically, opportunity is somewhat obvious and many are able to see it. They say that opportunity "knocks" or "calls" to us. In some way, it makes itself known!

Possibility, on the other hand, remains largely unnoticed and unannounced. People typically walk right by it and are almost stunned when someone else discovers it.

It does not make itself known because:

Possibility ... You have to see it in order to redeem it!

History teaches us that it is the ***"possibility-seekers"*** who make the greatest impact! They see what others do not see and as a result, they do what others never even imagined doing!

These are the people who see *solutions* where others only see a *struggle*. They see *ideas* where others only see *impossibility*. They launch *initiatives* out of *things that others left behind*.

You see, the point is that almost anyone can take advantage of opportunity ... but possibility ... well, possibility needs a seeker! Someone who can instinctively see what others cannot see, who will come pursuing with pure intentions in their heart and who will be determined to push through.

Possibility ... You have to see it in order to redeem it!

In all that we do, this is a reality we want to embrace. Developing the capacity to see possibility and having the determination to redeem it, assures that we fully redeem all that should be redeemed and that we put everything in play that should be put in play.

Possibility ... You have to see it in order to redeem it!

So what do you see anyway?

There has to be something ... there just has to be!

RENEWED
"Living renewed" is better than "starting anew!"

At the dawning of every new year, there is a sense of newness that inspires thoughts of new potential to be enjoyed, new possibilities to be embraced, and new progress to be experienced!

Because the awareness of these things is so obvious for us to see, we always begin the new year with expectation, and in some way, we seek to find a way to engage with all that is promised.

We set goals, we make resolutions, and we target changes that we should make. Even if we do not do these things … we think about them … because the reality of *"starting anew"* is a dominating reality. It breeds hope, it energizes us and it gives us life!

I love all of these things, and I am an avid *"starting anew"* person!

But …

As much as the magic of the moment inspires us, generally, once the "new" wears off … all the good intentions fall away and tragically, the year becomes painfully ordinary. Though still rich in potential, possibilities and the promise of progress …. we end up living in all too familiar routines.

There is something we can do … and here it is!

We start believing this …

You know what is better than "starting anew?" … "Living renewed!!"

Once we shift our thinking, we can shift our focus from …

◊   *Expectation to execution*

◊   *Dreamy plans to daily priorities*

◊   *Talking about change to taking on the challenge of change*

When we do these things we move from "starting anew" to "LIVING RENEWED" … and that changes everything!

We will see goals realized, resolutions fulfilled and targets met!

This is my desire for the new year … and it is my hope for you as well!

Let's go for it!

CHALLENGES
They strengthen us.
We all need them.

I love international churches ... so you can easily conclude that I also love international communities, congregations ... and most of all international leaders!

They are my tribe! I get them and they get me!

We laugh at the same stories, are puzzled by the same behaviors and are impacted by the same challenges!

The stories are funny, the behaviors are odd and the challenges are difficult and yet ...

Challenges ... We all need them!

The truth is that challenges stretch us, strengthen us and ... in an odd way they serve us!

Now, I am not saying that we like them!

The truth is we seek to avoid them at all costs ... but the fact remains that they do change us in every way!

Challenges ... We all need them!

So here's to *embracing*, *enjoying* and *employing* challenges!

Can you get your head around what I am saying and that I am actually suggesting you do the same!

I hope so ... I really do!

So here's to ...

Challenges ... We all need them!

SURRENDER
What's your choice?
Stress, stretch, or surrender?

Recently I had several opportunities to be reminded of just how important it is to make great life choices when things spin out of control and the pressure is on.

Schedules that were stressful, decisions that were disappointing and conversations that became confrontational ... just to name a few of the things that have challenged me directly or indirectly this week.

None of us need to be reminded that we are not in control and all of us sincerely struggle when things start collapsing.

The fact of the matter is that in times like these we have three choices ....

Stress, stretch or ... surrender!

When things begin to spin out of control, those really are the options that we must choose between.

If we do not have a plan in place, then we will live with stress! Challenges come, difficulties develop and we are stressing! It is absolutely guaranteed to happen!

Stress, stretch or ... surrender!

We can also choose to stretch or be flexible. Honestly, that is a great way to live. Sadly, however, that can leave us feeling like we are being pulled apart ... like *Stretch Armstrong*. Do you remember Stretch?

Stretch Armstrong was an action figure that was conceived and developed by Bill Armasmith and was in production from 1976 until 1980. I cannot say that I am all that familiar with him but let's be honest, who can forget the shape of a short, well-muscled blonde man wearing a black speedo. Some of you are moaning already!

The doll's most notable feature was that it could be stretched from its original size (about 15 inches) to four or five feet.

On many days, I have wished that I was Stretch and maybe you have as well.

If you can't stretch ... you are going to stress!

Stress, stretch or ... Surrender!

Then there is that third option ... the one that God calls us to embrace!

I can choose to make a willful decision that I am going to develop the discipline of surrender. I accept that God is in control, that He is at the center of it all and that I can confidently put my trust in Him. I surrender to Him knowing that He will take care of me ... in all things and at all times.

We need not live our lives under the tyranny of stress or in allowing life to stretch us completely out of shape and pull us apart.

We can choose surrender ... to Him, to His control and to His Lordship over us.

Stress, stretch or ... surrender!

What will it be?

I know what I want to choose!

I am going to say good-bye to stress, so long stretch (and to *Stretch Armstrong* for that matter) and say hello to surrender.

There really is no better way!

KEY INSIGHTS

- ◊ *If we're naturally-minded, our eyes will not see what's possible. But if we spiritually condition our inner person, we will be able to quest after new possibilities.*
- ◊ *Living in a consistent state of renewal is better than just starting something new.*
- ◊ *We welcome challenges. Why? Because they are change agents.*
- ◊ *Yielding and surrendering to our Father is the best posture in every situation. It positions us for the best outcomes.*

PRAYER AND AFFIRMATION

Father, forgive me for my insensitivity. You are a good God, and your glory fills the earth. Open the eyes of my understanding. Heal my vision. Today is an acceptable time for me ... it is a day salvation (2 Corinthians 6:2) ... a time of renewal. Thank you for strength to overcome every challenge. Thank you for the transformation which you supply. Spirit of God, I yield to your leading in all things. I get out of the way so you can fill up that space. Christ is a winner, and I'm a winner in Christ. Amen.

ADVANCING FORWARD

What is that one thing today, however small, that you can see and pursue? Everything begins with one little step. Beginning today, recondition yourself to think, see, and pursue possibilities! Be sensitive to the renewal of the Holy Spirit. Embrace every challenge in faith. Resolve afresh that you will yield to God.

RESTORE
Hope restored makes all the difference.

Daily we are reminded that our world is more complex, complicated and compromised than ever before.

So many sad things have happened so fast, in so many places that skepticism prevails, sincere trust has been shattered and the sense of desperation is growing stronger.

In the face of this disturbing trend, it is very clear that we need to be about the business of ...

Restoring hope!

Today we face extreme pressure to stay current, efficient and relevant in all that we say and do!

- ◊ *We need to be increasingly intentional about our awareness of the real needs of those around us, and about our activity in our communities.*
- ◊ *We need to be powerful proclaimers of carefully crafted messages of hope.*
- ◊ *We need to determinedly demonstrate that those who hope in the Lord will never be disappointed.*

Restoring hope!

The fact is that the one who has hope has everything!

Knowing all of this makes the promise of Isaiah 40:31 all the more meaningful for us and for our world.

"But those who hope in the Lord will renew their strength. They will soar on wings like eagles; they will run and not grow weary, they will walk and not be faint" (Isaiah 40:31).

Restoring hope!

To this we are called, for this we are challenged, and in this we find our common commitment.

I am in ... how about you?

EXPECTATION
Hopeful expectation elevates everyone and everything.

This is a very special moment for our family!

Our little granddaughter, Hannah Michelle, came into our world and quickly into our hearts! She joined her twin brothers Caleb and Luke and is the perfect addition to our family.

Anticipating her arrival, thinking about how great it would be to have a little girl in my life again, wondering what she would look like and who she would take after heightened my awareness of just how powerful "hopeful expectation" can be!

The wonderful thing about hopeful expectation is ...

- ◊ *It nurtures a positive perspective!*
- ◊ *It keeps you out of the funk!*
- ◊ *It promotes a deep longing in your heart!*
- ◊ *It gives you life!*

I am being reminded that "hopeful expectation" is powerful at so many levels ... and that it is good for us!

We need to look for things that provoke and produce "hopeful expectation" and embrace them fully.

Equally, we need to remember that we are designed to be "people of hope," so nurturing "hopeful expectation" in our lives and in the lives of others is the right thing to do!

I can tell you that what I am feeling in my heart is something that I want everyone to experience!

The wonderful thing about hopeful expectation is ...

Well ... each of us will answer that differently, but every expression will be life-giving, full of joy and so good for the soul!

Baby Hannah has already impacted us and she is only one week old!!

Pretty amazing huh!

BIRTHING
Resolve that you will birth hope into our world.

The new year is only one week old … and I trust it has opened well for you! I know that being prepared to redeem it is a challenge … but the fact is that if we do not redeem it, we will regret it!

My personal practice is to begin the new year with a renewed spiritual focus that is born out of a freshly revealed scriptural focus.

I am very excited about the specific focus that the Lord has given me for this year which is …

Building hope into our hearts … birthing hope into our world.

My sense is that in the same way that doubt diminishes faith, and unforgiveness diminishes prayer … lack of hope diminishes belief! It should be no surprise to us that our world breeds doubt, unforgiveness and lack of hope. These things are rampant in today's society!

Now more than ever, we need hope to come powerfully to us so that we can personally birth it into the hearts of others. Making this a reality, no matter what it requires of us is the only real choice we have.

Building hope into our hearts … birthing hope into our world.

This is a desperate need in our world and dealing with it is the desired activity of our God!

We who are His sons and daughters need to be filled with hope … and allow hope to flow from us to others!

I am looking forward to digging into all of this! I know where my focus will lie in the new year … how about you?

If you are seeking, He is speaking … and whatever He says to you … do it!

I am on it … how about you?

PROMOTE
Intentionally and strategically promote your hope.

Many phrases have been crafted to communicate what is required to create community ... but this one works for me!

Promote your hope!!

We all desire to engage with positive people, to do things that are profitable and to be a part of initiatives that prosper.

Making this a possibility ... well, that is where things get a little problematic! Well actually, they get a lot problematic! Knowing this, one of the best things that you can do is to ...

Promote your hope!!

Make it a point to talk openly and often about what you hope to see established among those that you love and lead. Articulate what you dream about, anticipate that others will want to participate with you and activate an intentional plan of implementation.

In order to do these things you will need to:

◊   *Think strategically* — make sure that your language is clear, convincing and communicates your hope and vision well.

◊   *Talk specifically* — use your created language in every way possible ... print it, post it and publicize it!

◊   *Train systematically — initiate a step-by-step plan that engages, empowers and employs others.*

Promote your hope!!

It works ... and because it does, we can indeed develop what we dream of and hope for in every way.

When that happens ... things get better really fast, life renews and hope reigns!

Works for me ... how about you?

Promote your hope!!

Key Insights

- *If you have hope, you have everything. Intentionally restore hope in others to lift their expectation.*
- *Hopeful expectation is a seedbed of an extraordinary life and career/ministry. It's an "elevating force" for good!*
- *Consistently carry hope within. And then give birth to it ... for yourself and others. Release life!*
- *Promote your hope. "Publish" hope. Herald hope. As you do, you will creatively impact those within your sphere of influence.*

Prayer and Affirmation

Father, I praise you, for you are the "God of hope," and you fill me with all joy and peace in believing, that I may abound in hope by the power of the Holy Spirit (Romans 15:13). Fill me with your hope. I say that my faith is the "substance," the assurance of all that I hope for (Hebrews 11:1). I seek to filter out anything that would seek to drain hope from my life and work. I clothe myself in the hope of Jesus Christ. Thank you, Father. Make me an "evangelist of hope." Amen.

Advancing Forward

What are those "forces" that are draining hope from your life and work? Can you discern them? Seek to filter these things. Intentionally seek and receive the hope of God in increasing measure. Sow hope into others and into other contexts. You will reap what you sow. Know that you are designed to be a hope-filled creation in Christ.

MAX
Learning what matters most and living it to the max!

When we live focused on purpose, fervent in passion and faithful in priority ... we make the most of the days that lie before us!

We dare not waste time or simply spend it. Our desire should be to invest it. As wise stewards.

Learning what matters most ... and living it to the max!!

I want to encourage you to determine in your heart to live in this way.

Every year I establish a dominant message that becomes my specific aim. I seek to discover what can be learned, and I struggle with the depth of what is being spoken.

The message for this year is ... you guessed it ...

Learning what matters most ... and living it to the max!!

What will drive my study is this verse from the prophet Micah ... *"But he's already made it plain how to live, what to do, what God is looking for in men and women. It's quite simple: Do what is fair and just to your neighbor, be compassionate and loyal in your love, And don't take yourself too seriously—take God seriously"* (Micah 6:8).

I am on a mission, I am already investigating, I am ready to learn ... and to make this year count in every way.

Every day is ours to redeem ... so let's get on with it!

Learning what matters most ... and living it to the max!!

SOWING
The truth remains:
you reap what you sow.

Here is a reality I'm confident you've heard many, many times before ... *"You reap what you sow!"*

This is not a *Zig Ziglar Zinger* or a *Maxwell Maxim*. It's straight from the Word of God! (Galatians 6). And it's a wholly biblical principle. It is eternally true and entirely trustworthy!

We need to hear this again and again:

This truth remains ... you reap what you sow!

Funny how often we forget the obvious!

The application of this principle can work for us ... or against us! We decide that for ourselves, and the principle simply delivers what we decide. We honestly cannot be surprised or pretend we did not know because ....

This truth remains ... you reap what you sow!

I experience the good and the bad of this truth all the time in my own life. I see it being played out in the lives of others as well.

My greatest joys and deepest sorrows are the results of seeing this principle being executed ... in me and in others! We would be wise to take this truth deep into our hearts, and then to examine every movement and motive based on this principle.

To intentionally start sowing based on what we want to reap ... this is the one and only way to assure we become all He desires us to become, receive all He wants us to receive and do all He wants us to do!

This truth remains ... you reap what you sow!

So let's mark this, mentor this and make this our life passion, pattern and priority! This is and will remain ... *eternally true and entirely trustworthy!*

WORTH
Are the things you are living for worth dying for?

Confrontational conversations, provocative ponderings ... are not generally things that we race to embrace! It happens and we take it on, but seriously do not want to do it again. In reality, we avoid these things because they disquiet us and make us feel uncomfortable.

However, the truth is that we need pushy people in our lives! Those who dare to take us on, call us out and demand that we live, look and lead as dynamic Christ-followers. People who ask tough questions knowing that they transform us.

The first such question that I remember being asked is this one ...

Are the things you are living for worth dying for?

I was 16 when someone asked me that question and it troubled me because I knew deep down I was getting it wrong. Of course, I could never admit I was troubled, or scared, so I simply called the question stupid. Not a very imaginative thing to do ... then, or now!

In the end, this question provoked me to action and I got busy seeking to shift my situation and to fix whatever needed fixing in my life.

This one question changed a lot in me ... and for me!

This week I was asked another provocative question by Royce Bervig who serves with *Focus On The Family* in Major Gift Planning Development.

Remember ... my first question was ...

Are the things you are living for worth dying for?

Now I have another question looming over me and demanding I reckon with it!

Royce's question to me was this ... **I know that you know about living in grace, but do you know about living for eternity?** He then shared how this question shifted everything for him! He was 50 when he was asked the question, and once he heard it, he immediately knew he had to make a major life change.

As I listened to Royce, I knew the same thing was being required of me. Another life vision development step awaits me ... and I must take it on!

My prayer is that as you read this, you will know it is required of you as well.

We all need confrontational conversations and provocative ponderings ... we just do!

My prayer is that your heart will be moved by these things as well. Take this on, make the change and look for favor, because it will come to you ... it surely will!

Hear these questions again ...

- ◊ "Are the things you are living for worth dying for?"
- ◊ "I know that you know about living in grace ... but do you know about living for eternity?"

Think about it! Really, really think about it!

FOCUS
Focus drives our lives, and we decide where to focus.

My focus needs to shift and I know it.

I guess part of my reality is that I am holding on to the past because I know it all too well, while the new year ahead is entirely unknown. While it does feel safe at some level, it is a seriously risky position for me or anyone else to be in.

We have to *"focus forward"* … there is no other way!

Here is a principle that we want to embrace …

Focus is what drives our lives … and we decide where we focus!

I understand the hesitancy we have in embracing something new! We have no idea as to what it will bring us.

- ◊ *Will it be kind or cruel?*
- ◊ *Will I face new challenges or find new opportunities?*
- ◊ *Will I be negatively pushed to my limits or be positively promoted beyond measure?*

Since we cannot know the answers to questions like this, we hesitate!

The fact of the matter is that …

Focus is what drives our lives … and we decide where we focus!

We move forward because we focus on things that *promote life*, *redeem opportunities* and *empower us to stay positive*. These things are always present but are often passed over because we become pulled away and allow other things to become our point of focus.

We concentrate on the lesser things when we could have been captured by the greater.

Real challenges and rich opportunities always co-exist and often feed off of each other … and we get to decide which one drives us.

If our focus is on the lesser things, we will live fatigued, frustrated and forever loathing about small things. If we focus on the greater things, we will live in fullness, fully satisfied and forever longing for more of His rich abundant favor.

Focus is what drives our lives … and we decide where we focus!

Knowing this makes it clear we need to decide to keep our focus on task. We will know when we get it right because we will live in a place of favor!

Living focused and looking forward!

That's my plan … how about you?

Key Insights

- ◊ *Discover and then fix your mind on what matters most in each situation. Every opportunity. And then hit your maximum level by living full out!*

- ◊ *The Creator has designed the law of sowing and reaping into all things. The law of the harvest is never mocked! (Galatians 6:7-8). Use it advantageously.*

- ◊ *What is worthy of your life? Another question is, "What is worth dying for?" The answers provide clear clues for your life-focus.*

- ◊ *The power of focus is a key driver in your life. Use Spirit-given discernment to make quality decisions and then focus hard!*

Prayer and Affirmation

Father, continuously show me what matters most. From week to week, and season to season. Energize me to run my race to win (1 Corinthians 9:24-27). I will use the law of harvest for Kingdom advantage in my life. Reveal to me, Holy Spirit, the true worth of my life. I resolve to make Spirit-inspired decisions. And then focus with strength! Thank you, Father, for the privilege of partnering with you in your Kingdom. Amen.

Advancing Forward

For each situation, opportunity, and season, clearly determine what matters most. Then, resolve to go full out! Do a personal audit of the law of sowing and reaping in your life. What is it saying? What changes can you make? Invest some time and record in your journal what's worthy of your life. Be intentional and strategic. Think through how you can harness your ability to focus on making things better. Concentrate your vision, prayers, and activity in new ways.

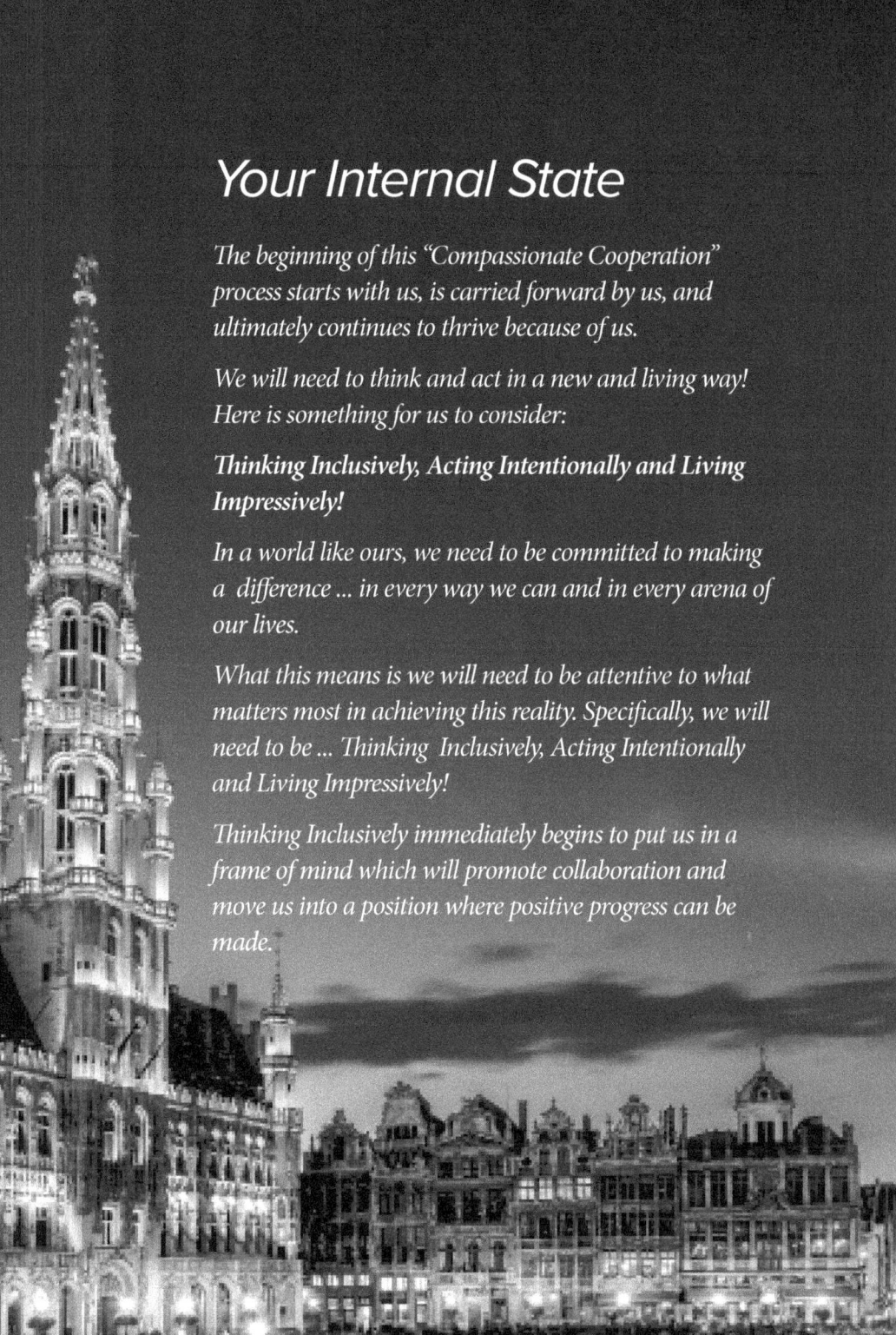

Your Internal State

The beginning of this "Compassionate Cooperation" process starts with us, is carried forward by us, and ultimately continues to thrive because of us.

We will need to think and act in a new and living way! Here is something for us to consider:

Thinking Inclusively, Acting Intentionally and Living Impressively!

In a world like ours, we need to be committed to making a difference ... in every way we can and in every arena of our lives.

What this means is we will need to be attentive to what matters most in achieving this reality. Specifically, we will need to be ... Thinking Inclusively, Acting Intentionally and Living Impressively!

Thinking Inclusively immediately begins to put us in a frame of mind which will promote collaboration and move us into a position where positive progress can be made.

It's amazing to see how much difference this makes! Take note of what your frame of mind is as you approach new situations and see if you are in fact ... thinking inclusively!

Acting intentionally will enable you to fully redeem the potential that comes from thinking inclusively. There will be no loss of momentum because you are acting intentionally. This leads you into a position of consensus building. You will find a way to engage every asset that is available to you. Decisions are easily made because ... in acting intentionally there is greater clarity and clearer communication.

Living impressively comes easily because of the process we have engaged. When we put collaboration in place and promote consensus-building, we will provide the context for crafting community. And once we create healthy community, all that we do becomes more impressive, simply because we are doing it together! As we are in community with others who are positive, focused and connected, great things will happen!

In a world like ours, we need to be committed to making a difference ... and when we are, the results are powerfully positive. And that changes everything!

This is a good thing ... a very good thing!

Personal Reflection

ENCOURAGING RELATIONAL EXCHANGE

"Compassionate Cooperation" ... A process that begins with enriching your heart, thus encouraging relational exchange and engaging your collective capacity.

The Father, Son, and Holy Spirit are highly relational. The intimate community of the Godhead placed the image of God in a man and woman … the most intimate of relationships. See the principle at creation. Relationships are a high value with God and are directly connected with His image. Every type of relationship matters to God. Authentic leadership flows from the heart, through the context of our relational life, and into our leadership function.

CONNECTION
Creating connection is the call.
Committed to community.

The Continental Theological Seminary (CTS) Faculty/Staff Retreat is an annual gathering where our CTS team comes together to diligently prepare for a new academic year. We share significant details, make strategic decisions, and most of all, we seek for clear spiritual direction!

Our desire is to see His destiny being fulfilled in every way and being fully revealed in every heart!

In order for this to be accomplished, we know that we must be intentional about everything that we say and do!

My specific word of challenge to our team was centered on this reality ...

Creating connection is the call ... crafting community is the commitment!

This matters for so many reasons but here is what specifically moves our team. We know that *"connection facilitates the discipleship/life development process and community fashions that reality!"*

Because of what we are dreaming of and what we deeply desire the Lord to do on our campus, we are intentionally beginning with the end in view!

We want supernatural visitation and we long for spiritual victories, so we will stand valiantly with our hearts and hope anchored in Him.

Creating connection is the call … crafting community is the commitment!

We are taking this on ... and perhaps you need to do the same?

It could be that you, in your context and community, are longing for the same things that we long for at CTS?

So ... if this is true, "Say Yes" to ...

Creating connection is the call … crafting community is the commitment!

Take the journey with us!

Come on ... what are you waiting for?

A DIFFERENCE
Coming together to make it happen.

I recently spent time talking and interacting with people who are completely committed to making a difference.

Each person talked passionately about their concern for specific issues that they knew would have to be addressed intentionally and they were determined to engage ... and to enlist the support of everyone they encountered.

As I listened to them share, it became immediately obvious that they not only had intense passion, they also had an inspired plan to enact ... and that is exactly what it takes to move things forward.

At the core of each plan was this networking reality ...

Making a difference ... come together to make it happen!

There is nothing more critical to the change process than this reality!

We cannot take on challenging concerns individually. Difficult decisions require the building of consensus and the art of negotiating.

Now, more than ever, we need to see these things happen!

Posturing around personal agendas, insisting on individual fulfillment, or seeking to build your own kingdom will always be the demise of securing real change.

These are days of unprecedented opportunity!

It is, however, couched in the midst of unbelievable obstacles. Thus, we will be required to mine out the potential that exists in every problem. This will test the depth of our capacity in every way.

Making a difference ... come together to make it happen!

This is the call that we must answer, the commitment that we must accept .. and there is no way to avoid the cost of it all.

Making a difference ... come together to make it happen!

I am in ... how about you?

EXCHANGE
Trading "mine" for "ours."
One great exchange!

I enjoyed being a part of a historic gathering where a room full of very passionate individuals made a heroic decision!

◊   *When given the choice they decided to exchange personal agenda for powerful agreement.*

◊   *They decided that "we" is better than "me," and that "shared ministry" is better than "solo ministry".*

Trading "mine" for "ours" ... one great exchange!

Sadly, too many people fail to see this reality, and as a result, we deny possibilities and diminish potential! So many great things are lost because we cling to the good things.

Admittedly, this is a lot of risk ... but ...

The fact is that you have to "give to receive" and "lose to win."

Trading "mine" for "ours" ... one great exchange!

Those I was with got it right! They took the brave steps and there is no doubt that "greater things are yet to come!"

Trading "mine" for "ours" ... one great exchange!

Are you ready to take this on? I hope so because "your" best effort can only be seen in "our" expression!

NURTURE
Reaching to connect.
   Cultivating closeness.

Ruthanne and I are enjoying a season that is ***"intentionally-focused"*** on family, friends and faithful partners ... and we are loving every moment we are sharing with others! We are speaking in churches, having personal meetings, initiating phone conversations ... and we remain open to any other possible opportunity. We are meeting with people all day, every day ... with one great desire in our hearts ...

Nurturing relational closeness and connection!

We know that we have been enabled to serve as we do in Europe *(and now beyond Europe)* because others have been called to serve with us! Our prayer, relational and financial support all come from people who choose to invest in us and that is deeply humbling for sure ... but it also compels us to want to invest in them.

Nurturing relational closeness and connection!

Here is what we do to make this happen ...

- ◊ We make a prayer covenant to provide a prayer covering.
- ◊ We make a plan to communicate via emails, letters, phone calls and social media.
- ◊ We make a priority commitment to dedicate time to connect personally.

Taking these steps enables us to demonstrate our determination to stay close and connected. And that matters to us ... and I know it matters to you as well!

So ... let's do our very best to ...

- ◊ *Show honor to whom honor is due!*
- ◊ *Give as has been given to us!*
- ◊ *Care for those who care for us!*

In doing this we are doing what will bring increased blessing and favor to us from God ... and from others!

Nurturing relational closeness and connection!

I am all in on this one ... how about you?

Key Insights

- *If you want to actually experience the vision, some of your most important skills as leaders are creating connections and crafting community.*

- *There are immense challenges today. We also have great opportunities. The key, though, is that we come together with others to seize the opportunities.*

- *"Agreement" is exponentially stronger than "solo." Strong leadership realizes exchanging "mine" for "ours" is a winning proposition.*

- *As a vinedresser would "nurture" the vine, so we must intentionally nurture connections and relational closeness. Understand that true fruitfulness is organic and relationally-based.*

Prayer and Affirmation

Father, you are the Ultimate Connector and Community Builder. Equip me in this area. Transform me with the revelation that I can only fully seize opportunities you provide as I'm in alignment with others. I exchange "mine" for "ours." And I'm much stronger for it. Inspire me to nurture connections and community. My model is nothing less than the community between the Father, Son, and Holy Spirit. Let it be. All glory to you.

Advancing Forward:

Here's how you can begin to activate this now. Ask yourself this question: who are 3 people I can connect or re-connect with? Simply jot down the ones who instantly come to mind. God will use your own understanding to speak to you. Then, reach out today with a text, email, or call Maybe follow up with a coffee, lunch or walk. Intentionally change your mindset to one of "agreement" instead of "solo." Resolve that in the next meeting or planning session you lead, you will transition the atmosphere from hierarchy to collaboration.

KINDNESS
Everything can be nurtured
and moved toward positivity.

Today I listened to another message on *kindness*. And I was reminded again that ...

Kindness nurtures ... nearly everything!

There are numerous little sayings that underscore the importance of kindness. The biblical declaration in I Corinthians 13:4 begins by reminding us that *"Love is patient, love is kind ..."*

The speaker today made this statement:

"Kindness nurtures gratitude ... and gratitude nurtures surrender."

His point was that when we begin with kindness, with a positive action ... we will reap a positive reaction. And that positive reaction makes positive movement possible.

We live in a very divisive society, and often, when frustration prevails, we can become forceful in making our point and provoking people to respond. The fact is, that approach will not result in anything positive. Nothing at all!

The fact of the matter is that ...

Kindness nurtures ... nearly everything!

Now more than ever, all of us need to be committed to kindness. In word and deed ... we need to intentionally speak and show kindness.

In ministry, we need to proactively model and mentor kindness. In doing this, we set ourselves and others up to succeed. We nudge people to be kind and to be positive.

Greatest of all, by promoting kindness, we position ourselves and others to succeed, to be at peace and to live in a way that enables us to receive His very best!

Kindness nurtures ... nearly everything!

This is a response that I want to embrace.

How about you!

CONNECTIONS
Keep connecting. Expect exponential increase.

As I write this I am in Hong Kong making new relational connections ... and I love it!!

The ease at which these connections can be made is surprising, and the exponential value they add is stunning!

In every case, I am either creating new streams of relational support, or I am confirming that the connections that we have made in the past are indeed exactly what we hoped they would be!

It seems we are strategically positioned to accomplish all that we desire to accomplish!

Relational connections ... keep them going!

I want to encourage you to keep building new relational connections! The more connected we are ... the more we can excel at the things that we do.

Our dream for our team becomes stronger, our possibilities increase and we are enabled to do even more!

The fact is that what we are trying to achieve will require our best efforts in every way. So keep connecting ... and never stop!

Relational connections. Keep them going!

This is how to win.

And win big!

WORDS
Team words inspire teamwork and take us beyond.

I have just finished an inspiring week working closely with the extended *Convoy of Hope* team. Hearing the stories of how they serve, listening to the reports of their activities, and having the opportunity to get to know some of them personally, has made me intensely aware that this is one amazing team!

Our *Convoy* team is comprised of employees, interns, missionaries, partners, volunteers … and their levels of devotion, desire and dedication are equal across every sector. There was no distinguishable difference. Every person I encountered was passionately engaged!

What I was immediately aware of is that this kind of commitment is based on covenant. These individuals have made covenant with God, with themselves and with each other … and that takes them beyond!

As I have considered all that I observed this week, what I came away with is this … what is verbalized among and to team members matters! We need to be intentional about speaking and sharing.

Team words that inspire teamwork … and takes us beyond!

I know we often think about speaking positive words of affirmation that nurture positive attitudes. And that is a powerful action to initiate. However, there is something more powerful!

Team words that inspire teamwork … and takes us beyond!

It seems to me that speaking words that promote covenant will take us deeper, and we will begin to think about an alliance being established. This will give us a relational connection that will take us beyond just coming together for projects and move us to serving together with a purpose … and that position is perfect!

Team words that inspire teamwork … and takes us beyond!

I took notes this week and I also took my first steps in speaking to my team from **another level**. I have always been very intentional about doing my best to inspire teamwork. But now I want to speak words that take my team into covenant.

My sense is that this will make all we do together more than it has ever been … and I know this will bring good to all those involved.

This shift is going to serve me well! How about you … are you in?

CLOSE
Stay close to God and others. You never know what's coming.

This month I was made acutely aware of just how important it is for us to ...

Stay close ... to God and others! Because you never know what is coming!

News came from two dear friends who were suddenly faced with overwhelming circumstances. At the same time, Ruthanne and I were facing tough challenges as well!

The fact is these moments are more than we can face alone ... but the good news is that we are not alone, and if we are *staying close*, we instantly sense that reality!

I can assure you that support poured out to my two friends. And Ruthanne and I felt it as well!

It is critical for all of us to ...

Stay close ... to God and others! Because you never know what is coming!

I want to urge you to do whatever you need to do to draw near today ... to God and to those God has given to be with you!

This may be the time for us to put some things in order ... in our hearts and in our relationships!

Stay close ... to God and others! Because you never know what is coming!

Believe me, it is worth it!

KEY INSIGHTS

- ◊ *Kindness is an outworking of love. As we practice kindness, it creates positive reactions ... the kind of movement we are desiring.*

- ◊ *"Kingdom currency" flows on Kingdom connections. Initiate new and accurate connections. Then nurture these connections.*

- ◊ *Cultivate a "language" which cultivates teams. Realize that your words can create good and worthy realities.*

- ◊ *God has given us the "ministry of reconciliation." This includes being reconciled to one another. Closeness is good for us and what we do.*

PRAYER AND AFFIRMATION

Father, hope does not disappoint as your love is shed abroad in our hearts by your Spirit (Romans 5:5). Fill me with your love and kindness. Connect me with the right people, at the right time, in the right places—I desire accuracy. Fill my heart and mouth with language which creates unity. May my heart overflow with warmth to others ... the heart sentiment of Jesus. I thank you. Amen.

ADVANCING FORWARD

Initiate acts of kindness, however small. Prime the "kindness pump" with decisions and acts of your will that bless and benefit others. Look for a flow of kindness to be released. Reach out to establish new relationships. Connect in new and fresh ways. Ask the Holy Spirit to show you how to be close to others. He will teach you. After all, the Holy Spirit, the Son, and the Father share infinite closeness in the Godhead. Heaven wants something of that to flow in the Body of Christ. It will happen if you ask for it and lean into it.

SUPPORT
Jesus calls us to support and empower the weak.

Perhaps it's the season that is making us increasingly aware of the fragility of so many people, or maybe we are just running into 'special situations' that capture our attention?

It is true that during Christmas we do see a lot of appeals for people in need and that many people struggle more during the Christmas season … but I really do not think this is the entire story!

The fact is that people are in need all year long and the struggle may intensify during Christmas … but it's always there!

I think what happens actually is that these are moments when we are reminded of the spiritual mandate we've been given to …

Support the weak!

Jesus in His words, and by His example, teaches us to seek out those in need! He ministered to those in pain. He responded to the cry of the desperate and He healed the brokenhearted!

Support the weak!

It's not a Christmas emotion … even though we may feel it most at Christmas time!

We do see the need in this season! We are increasingly aware of the fragility of so many people! We know there are 'special situations' that capture our attention. But we are convinced that it is more than that for sure!

This is our call and our mandate as well! It is something we are intended to feel and practice … every day of the year!

We know this is what we want to do! How about you?

Support the weak!

BELONGING
There is a joy in the security,
and satisfaction of belonging.

This was my first time in Chisinau, Moldova and yet I did not feel alone, in fact, I felt warmly welcomed!

You know why?

The joy of belonging!

You see I was invited to meet with an incredible group of European church leaders. I knew someone would meet me at the airport, take me to the hotel, make sure I had everything I needed. He would then take me back to the airport at the end of the event.

I did not know who any of these people would be, but I was certain they would be there because it was all a part of ...

The joy of belonging!

Now I can show you photos and tell you the names of the wonderful people who quickly became friends!

I am often in situations where the diversity of language and culture seem to dictate that meaningful connection is just impossible, and yet the bonds of belonging always prevail!

The joy of belonging!

I love that feeling. And I'm grateful I can experience it in ever-expanding levels in such a variety of ways!

However, I'm even more grateful that I can know the joy of belonging to God!

The promise to us is this: *"I am my Beloved's and He is mine" (Song of Solomon 6:3)*!

How amazing is that!

I belong to God and He belongs to me!

To know His warm embrace and tender care is beyond description!

I love the words of *I Stand In Awe Of You* by Hillsong United!

> *You are beautiful beyond description*
> *Too marvelous for words*
> *Too wonderful for comprehension*
> *Like nothing ever seen or heard*
> *Who can grasp your infinite wisdom*
> *Who can fathom the depth of your love*
> *You are beautiful beyond description*
> *Majesty enthroned above*
> *And I stand, I stand in awe of you*
> *I stand, I stand in awe of you*
> *Holy God to whom all praise is due*
> *I stand in awe of you.*

There is such *security, strength,* and *satisfaction* in knowing this and living in the reality of it!

The Joy Of Belonging ... the gift that keeps on giving! I am already looking forward to my next opportunity! How about you!

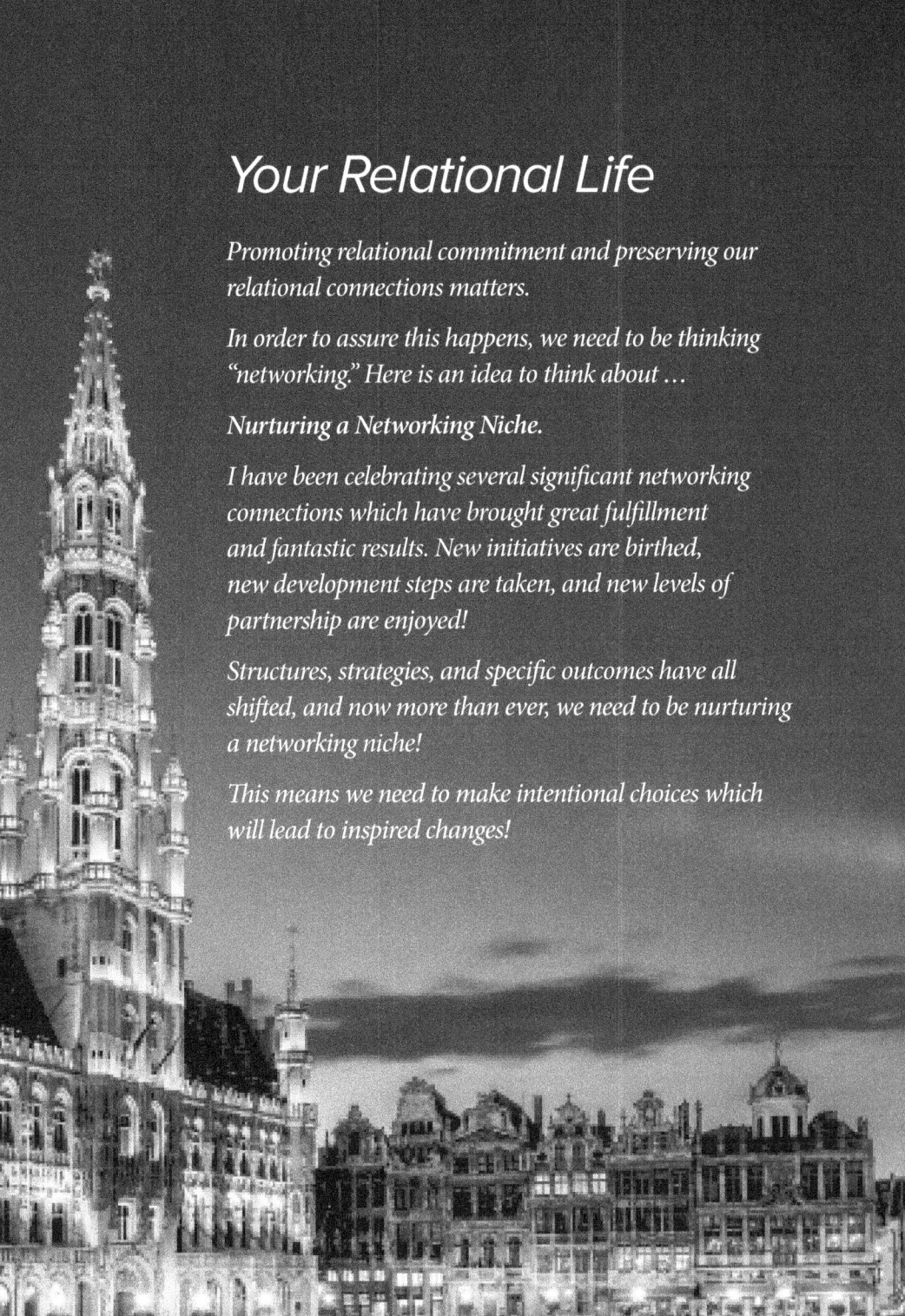

Your Relational Life

Promoting relational commitment and preserving our relational connections matters.

In order to assure this happens, we need to be thinking "networking." Here is an idea to think about …

Nurturing a Networking Niche.

I have been celebrating several significant networking connections which have brought great fulfillment and fantastic results. New initiatives are birthed, new development steps are taken, and new levels of partnership are enjoyed!

Structures, strategies, and specific outcomes have all shifted, and now more than ever, we need to be nurturing a networking niche!

This means we need to make intentional choices which will lead to inspired changes!

Here is how I would describe a great networker: "Individuals who are positive, passionate, proactive partners."

Positive — *people enjoy connecting with individuals who are positive in their approach.*

Passionate — *people enjoy connecting with individuals who are passionate about the way they live, the task they've been given, and the team which serves with them.*

Proactive — *people enjoy connecting with individuals who are proactive in engaging, encouraging, and enabling others.*

Partner — *people enjoy connecting with individuals who are committed to serving together, sharing together, and staying together ... no matter what!*

The individuals who nurture these values accelerate networking.

Doing this is right. It makes us ready and it releases ever-increasing levels of God's rich favor and fullness.

In the end ... everybody wins.

Personal Reflection

ENGAGING YOUR COLLECTIVE CAPACITY

"Compassionate Cooperation"...
A process that begins with
enriching your heart, thus
encouraging relational
exchange and engaging
your collective capacity.

Jesus is perfect theology. And he is a perfect leader. He models for us what true leadership is. There is a way that things work in life, business, and ministry. Jesus shows us that way. The leader is first a passionate Christ-follower and then provides a lead on an initiative or mission. If we yield, the Holy Spirit will develop in us the skill to lead with integrity, accuracy, and impact. It truly is a partnership between heaven and earth.

PRIORITIES
Prayer, priorities, and a plan.
A powerful process.

I am so excited about the opening of the new year for many reasons! I have already prayed over it, put priorities in place and prepared a plan to assure that these things come to pass.

All three of these steps are critical … but more importantly, unless all three are activated, nothing can be accomplished.

Prayer, priorities, and a plan … a powerful process!

The fact is that unless we do these things … chaos will prevail!

◊   *We will lack spiritual wisdom, so we will have to struggle with superficial wisdom.*

◊   *We will lack strategic priorities, so we will have to settle for self-made priorities.*

◊   *We will lack specific plans, so we will have to survive on scary plans that are crafted on a whim and executed on the run.*

We will struggle to make progress, to push thru challenges and to find a pathway to peace. While there may movement, there will not be meaningful activity!

Does any of this sound good to you? I seriously doubt it!

There is a better way and here it is!

Prayer, priorities, and a plan ... a powerful process!

When we live like this, amazing things happen for us ... and all of them are outstandingly good!

- ◊ We experience all the blessings that a life of prayer produces.
- ◊ We enjoy all the benefits of being focused and intentional.
- ◊ We embrace the beauty of His plans becoming our reality.

How does that sound to you? I seriously like it ... and I bet you do as well!

This is exactly how I want to live out the new year ... and my whole life for that matter!

Are you in? How could you not be!

This is how we win ... absolutely and in every way!

NEXT
Think "next steps" to pursue intentional development.

Making progress and experiencing intentional development are what we all long for in our own lives and in the lives of those we love and lead.

There is nothing dynamic about living a diminishing life or leading a declining ministry/organization!

So ... the fact of the matter is that ...

We have to be thinking next steps!

If not ... decline is inevitable and disappointments are inescapable!

"Thinking next steps" means that we are seeking specific direction, anticipating challenges before they catch us and are focused on fulfillment!

A 10-year plan will not save us ... but "projected" thinking will serve us well!

We have to be thinking next steps!

I want to encourage you to honestly evaluate yourself in this area!

- ◊ What do your **"long-term plans"** *look like really?*
- ◊ *Do they excite you?*
- ◊ *Will others be inspired by them?*

These are questions that we need to be asking ... and based on how we respond, we will know exactly how well we are doing!

We have to be thinking next steps!

There really is no other way to live and lead with distinction!

PLAN
A master plan or messy plans ... your call!

I am in a season of engaging in a new ministry initiative and as a result of that, I am prayerfully and busily crafting a "master plan."

I am seeking to identify what matters most, what must be pursued and what must be avoided. There is great safety in setting priorities in order, seeking proper perspective and staying in a strategic position.

None of these things happen by chance ... and quite frankly, here is the truth!

A master plan or messy plans ... your call!

Seriously, this is the bottom line!

If we do not make a plan, things will get messy!

It just happens ... all by itself!

I want to encourage you to take the time and exercise the discipline to lay out a plan of action for all the things that you want to do well ... whether they are personal, spiritual, relational, financial, work or ministry related ... MAKE A PLAN!

By praying, engaging, thinking and planning ... you will bring order to your life, clarity to your mind, and greatest of all, joyful fulfillment to your heart.

There is something quite powerful about living with purpose.

A master plan or messy plans ... your call!

Ignoring all of this will not just result in the loss of all of these beautiful things ... it will lead to one messy situation after another.

I cannot tell you how energized I feel as I am crafting my plan!

There is a keen sense of expectation growing in my heart!

The actions I am taking remove the risk of things getting messy and promote the possibility that this master plan is going lead to something utterly amazing!

A master plan or messy plans ... your call!

I know what I am going to do ... how about you?

You got it ... right?

EXCELLENCE
Are we messaging mediocrity or encouraging excellence?

Let me begin by stating clearly that we are making this choice day by day in all that we say and do! Like it or not, agree or disagree ... this is the reality!

It is impossible to be neutral on this one!

Massaging mediocrity or ... encouraging excellence!

Because this is true ... we do need to think about what we are doing! Our personal and professional lives are being impacted by the choices we make, as are the people we love and the places we serve!

We are either appealing for the best or applauding "second best."

Think about it!

There is divine potential in every heart and something to be redeemed in every situation. Our one and only task is to assure that these things happen!

So ... we have a critical commitment to consider, don't we?

Massaging mediocrity or ... encouraging excellence!

What will it be? What will we do?

The fact is that how I deal with myself will determine how I will deal with others!

It is time for all of us to take a deep look and to call out what we see. What are we doing? What does the evidence reveal?

Now more than ever we need to get this right!

Mediocrity is killing us and keeping us from being all that we are destined to be!

Let's be done with **"*massaging mediocrity*"** and determine that **"*encouraging excellence*"** is our first and final decision.

We will be better people because of this and we will build better people as well!

Massaging mediocrity or ... encouraging excellence!

I know what I am going to do ... how about you?

KEY INSIGHTS

- ◊ *Always start with prayer. Establish priorities. Then create a smart plan. This is the pathway to meaningful activity.*

- ◊ *Don't think "previous." Consistently think "next." Next thinking/projected thinking will serve us well.*

- ◊ *Things get messy by default. But a master plan sets the course and brings order and design to our life and work. Pray. Plan. Perform.*

- ◊ *Mediocrity is a thief and killer. Aim for excellence in all things ... personal, relational, and work/ministry. Excellence reveals God's nature and serves his purposes.*

PRAYER AND AFFIRMATION

Father, I resolve to pray, prioritize and plan ... all toward the goal of activity which pleases you. Help me to project my thinking outward. "Next thinking" is what I desire. Holy Spirit, illuminate me to create master plans which release your design. I put mediocrity behind me. Excellence is before me. I give glory to you, my Excellent God. Amen.

ADVANCING FORWARD

Level up by creating prayer-borne plans, however small. Just activate the process and habit. Grab a journal. Invite the Holy Spirit into the process, and then do some free writing, recording thoughts and concepts to move you in the direction of "next thinking." What's messy in your life and work? Begin to bring order to it. God is a God of order. Create a thematic journal focusing on excellence. Record goals, prayers and affirmations, and accomplishments in your pursuit of excellence.

DEADLINES
Overcoming the lingering dangers of deadline living.

All of us who live fully engaged lives know of the intimidating presence and the intense pressure that is produced by deadline living. We live in the reality of these things more than we should and know all too well that they take a toll on us. Tragically, we never seem to be able to escape this tyranny.

The lingering dangers of deadline living!

We are likely highly skilled in time management principles, know well how to prioritize our work and how to arrange our schedules … and yet still, all too often, we feel pressed into deadline living.

My sense is this is something we cannot eliminate or master, but rather is something we need to embrace and manage. We need to do this in great haste as there are classic dangers we will incur if we do not *"embrace and manage."*

I think it does us well to recount for ourselves what is at risk when we are driven by deadlines.

- ◊ *Our creativity to embellish our work is limited.*
- ◊ *Our capacity to express ourselves elegantly is lost.*
- ◊ *Our clarity in communication is lacking.*

Add to that the impact of stress, the drain of frustration and the loss of relationship that we suffer because we are living on the edge … and we can begin to see the crushing reality.

The lingering dangers of deadline living!

It can be different than this … there is, in fact, a better way and we need to find it for ourselves and freely help others figure out what they need to do as well.

Here is how we get there:

◊   *Counting the cost*
◊   *Calculating our choices*
◊   *Committing to change*

It is as easy as that to start the shift that will signal our success!

Say goodbye to life as it has been and hello to life as it was meant to be!

I am in … how about you?

Let me hear you say, "YES!"

PASSION
Passion produces by defining, uniting, and compelling us.

This week I have focused many of my personal thoughts and my coaching conversations with others on this idea ...

Passion pursued produces!

I know there has been a lot of discussion and books devoted to the idea that we should be *"purpose-driven."* And while I understand that thought process, the reality is we are best poised for powerful engagement when we are ... *"passion-driven, purpose-focused and principle-centered."*

The fact is that passion enables us to accurately discern our purpose and to actively develop a principle-centered life. Living like this enables us to satisfy the heart of our God and to succeed in life in every way!

When I say, "*Passion pursued produces,*" here is what I mean:

◊ **Passion pursued defines us** — *we begin to piercingly know who we are and what we do. Very little momentum is lost and we begin to be known by what passion defines for us!*

◊ **Passion pursued unites us** — *a commonly shared passion is the stuff of greatness! Teams come together faster, function at a higher level, projects are better organized, and thus are more effective in every way.*

◊ ***Passion pursued compels us*** — *a focus on passion ignites our hearts! We are consumed in a way that changes everything! There is a dynamic shift on the inside that drives and dominates ... and that makes all the difference in the world.*

REMEMBER, what defines us, will develop us ... and ultimately dominate every fiber of our being!

Passion pursued produces!

So keep passion always in front of you! There is no other way to live. Seriously!

I am all in ... how about you?

MISSION
If you do not have a clear mission, then all you have is a job.

One of the most strategic and significant things we can do is to craft a clear mission that gives us something to live for that really matters.

In faith, life, and ministry we need to prepare pathways that provide for ongoing development and involvement.

If you do not have a clear mission ... then all you really have is a job!

The fact is that we want to assure we are on mission and doing our very best to live out all that God has intended for us.

To live or serve at a lesser level not only diminishes our personal potential, it deters our personal progress and it destroys our personal peace of mind.

This may be a great time to re-evaluate the way you define and describe all you do in each of these three major arenas.

We are doing this right now and found these tips quite helpful as we began to engage in this process. Perhaps you will as well.

Include the four key elements of **value, inspiration, plausibility, and specificity!**

- ◊ *Keep it short*
- ◊ *Consider long-term vs. short-term*
- ◊ *Test it*
- ◊ *Revisit it often*

You can see more on this at: www.inc.com/ss/5-tips-on-developing-an-effective-mission-statement#0.

If you do not have a clear mission ... then all you really have is a job!

The reality is we can and should seek to be our best and do our best in all things and at all times!

We do not want a job ... so we are determined to stay on mission!

Are you with us?

PERFECT
A perfect plan is always progressively perfect.

A perfect plan. How many times have you prayed for that?

The situation is dire, the circumstances desperate, someone needs an answer, something has to change. And **everybody is looking to you for the perfect plan!**

Deep down everyone knows that in real life there are no magic moments, no fancy formulas, no easy exits ... there is simply a challenge to confront, and you need the perfect plan!

Here is what we have to know:

The thing about a perfect plan is it is always progressively perfect!

Read that again because it will become increasingly important to you!

Knowing this will save us from the agony and tyranny of so many things!

◊ *Self-dependency*

◊ *Self-deception*

◊ *Self-destruction*

If we take this task on thinking and acting as if it all depends on us ... we will be in real trouble. And things will get bad. Real fast!

So open up to the plan-creation process, be comfortable with the creation-chaos and accept that **consistent, calculated change** *is critical to the cycle of development.*

When you do this, a plan will come together ... and it will progressively be a perfect plan!

Our call is to fearlessly face every challenge, seeking a solution, praying for a plan and reminding ourselves that ...

The thing about a perfect plan is ... it is always progressively perfect!

Hold on to this thought because it will help you, and then you will be empowered to help others!

That works right?

KEY INSIGHTS

◊ *Tolerating chronic deadlines unleashes toxic stress and inhibits creativity and joy. We have to be fierce in battling the "tyranny of the urgent." It's worth the fight.*

◊ *Passion is raw energy and produces great effect. Imagine receiving more and more of the "zeal of the Lord" in a strategic and fruitful way!*

◊ *Cultivating a mission mindset is the only way to live and progress in your calling. Think more entrepreneurially.*

◊ *A plan is never perfect. But it can always be "progressively perfect." Keep your planning open to updates from above. "Not that I have already obtained it, or have already become perfect, but I press on ..." (Philippians 3:12).*

PRAYER AND AFFIRMATION

Father, you are not stressed. And you do not want your children to be stressed. Give me skill to overcome the "tyranny of the urgent." I desire the "zeal of the Lord." Father, give me your passionate heart more and more. I say that Christ is The Ultimate Entrepreneur. I follow you, Jesus, in developing a courageous mission-mindset. I submit my planning to the Council of Heaven. Give me updates from above whenever you want. Help me to be sensitive to your voice. Prompt to obey. I present myself to you as a vessel of honor (2 Timothy 2:20-21). Amen.

ADVANCING FORWARD

Develop strategic steps to move away from "deadline living." Make up your mind once and for all that you will not live this way. Ask yourself, "What would the zeal of the Lord really look like in my life?" What would change? Read a good book on building an entrepreneurial mindset. What mental and emotional skills do you need? Look at your recent planning. Lay it out before the Lord. Are there any updates?

COACH
Everyone needs a coach, a mentor, and an advocate.

Anytime I hear someone refer to themselves or someone else as being *"self-made,"* I always feel compelled to pry a little to discover who they will ultimately acknowledge as having influence in their lives.

The fact of the matter is that no one is *"self-made."* More than that, the best and brightest among us, the most generous and gracious among us, can almost instantly call the names of those who have made great investment in our lives!

It is wisdom to openly acknowledge we need a *Savior*, a *Redeemer* and a *Deliverer* ... and to equally embrace the fact that ...

Everyone needs a coach, a mentor, and an advocate!

In simple terms:

◊   We need a **coach to inspire**.

◊   We need a **mentor to instruct**.

◊   We need an **advocate to intervene**.

The sooner we grasp the utter necessity of these "life realities," the better it is for us!

It is then, and only then, that we can begin to live powerfully, fulfill our potential and truly become the best we can be!

Everyone needs a coach, a mentor, and an advocate!

It does matter that we are quick to see our need of Jesus and to confess we desperately need Him!

It is also critical that we know the names of those in our lives who have become a *coach*, *mentor*, and *advocate*!

Any hesitation here should be deeply concerning to us!

None of us can do it by ourselves ... and

Everyone needs a coach, a mentor, and an advocate!

Jonathan Hollis, Lois Stoots, Paul Ecker, Allen Ross, Al Perna, Francesco Toppi, Stig Hedström ... I am making my list and loving it!

How about you?

PRACTICE
Ask yourself: "Are you practicing what you're preaching?"

I think all of us have heard that old adage, *"Practice what you preach."*

It may be a bit Puritan sounding ... but it is good counsel nonetheless!

People expect us to do what we say! That is integrity is action and it validates our message! Nothing is more damaging for the church than for it to be discovered that our message of *"demonstration"* is not equal to our message of *"declaration!"*

All too often, the church is called out because of what is viewed as a "hypocritical" action or attitude.

Ask yourself ... are you practicing what you're preaching?

My daughter Kristi and her husband Andrew Lundgren are newly-appointed *Chi Alpha* missionaries and are working hard to launch a *Chi Alpha* initiative on the campus of *Northwestern University.*

They attend *Chicago Tabernacle* and love being a part of this vibrant community!

Recently they had an experience there that so powerfully spoke to them and to every single person that I have shared their story with.

This is a classic expression of what it means to **"practice what you preach,"** and you will easily see the impact of such actions.

Kristi writes:

"Well, I have to give this little "testimony." I left church in tears on Sunday because the teacher of the 4 and 5 yr. old Sunday school class came to us (also with tears in her eyes) saying she felt Luke just couldn't handle the class anymore. He's too overwhelmed with the activities, too much commotion (it's a big class), etc., etc. And would we consider putting him in the toddler room? Pretty stupid of me to be crying because I was the one who suggested he move to the toddler room in the first place. But, ya know....it just hits ya hard when someone else has tried their best, but they have to finally admit they can't handle your child.

"So, I emailed the Director of Children's Ministries to start the dialogue of just what will we do with Luke on Sunday mornings and Tuesday evenings when we are attending church.

"Well, tonight the director came to me and asked all kinds of questions about Luke. She genuinely listened for a long time about his diagnosis and his abilities and his needs. Then she tells me that the main teacher in the toddler room is a special education teacher and she is very excited to meet Luke. But ALSO that they have a volunteer who is studying special education now who wants to be Luke's personal "helper" while he is at church. She'll stay with him the whole time. So, if he likes the toddler room he can stay there, but if he wants to go back and join his peers, she'll go with him there and make sure he gets the attention he needs. The director said, 'It will take a little of your time, but we want you to come and teach us how to teach Luke. And let us know of any particular toys he likes and we will go buy them."

"They got all that figured out and in place since I emailed them on Sunday night.

Wow!! Feeling so loved and cared for!"

You see it, don't you?

These compassionate, committed leaders at *Chicago Tabernacle* dared to ask the question and in doing so they delivered a powerful message!

Ask yourself ... are you practicing what you're preaching?

I want to urge you to take this on!

In a world like ours, we need *authenticity, integrity,* and *intentionality* more than ever!

In all that you say and do ...

Ask yourself ... are you practicing what you're preaching?

May that answer always be a resounding, "YES"!

DIFFERENCE
In order to make a difference,
you have to make a decision.

In September I had the honor of engaging with a great church that invited us to participate in their annual mission convention.

I quickly realized that this church was intensely passionate about missions, meaningfully connected to their community and deeply committed to God and each other. As I expected, when I met with their key leaders/members, I saw these same values being vibrantly expressed in each of their lives and ministries. The purposes they value, the plans they make and the priorities they promote all powerfully focus on these realities.

Here's what I learned once again:

In order to make a difference ... you have to make a decision!

This church consistently lives out their core values because they stand united in the decision to make that happen!

They work hard together to assure that everything that needs to be done is done ... all the time, in every way.

I do not know all that they do, but I do know that for initiatives to thrive and for leaders to succeed, it will be necessary to take intentional actions and to make strategic decisions.

Here are three specific steps which must be taken:

- ◊ **Be Proactive** — *the challenge is to "make the most of every opportunity." To redeem every moment and to use them to make a difference! To nurture the core values and the commonly shared values we want to promote.*

- ◊ **Be Persistent** — *the challenge is to "make every effort." To be diligent to turn every task into a mission and every dream into a vision. This enables us to serve with true joy, great passion and to be increasingly effective.*

- ◊ **Be Positive** — *the challenge is to "make the music in your heart." To create a heart and an attitude that honors God and attracts others. We know that pleasing God brings His presence near, and that a positive, life-giving attitude draws people to us.*

These are the unchanging realities we want to embrace!

In order to make a difference ... you have to make a decision!

It will not happen by accident. It will require intentional action ... and the sooner we start, the sooner we will begin to enjoy the results!

Being with this church this week and seeing what they are doing, convinces me that I want this ... for myself and for you!

So take this on with me!

Will you?

STORIES
Take time to tell the stories and give God the glory.

I've just come from an amazing gathering where participants are gathered from 120 nations and though there are many things that could divide us, we are celebrating what unites us … a commonly shared faith experience that captivates, a common sense of mission that compels and a common bond of partnership that connects us.

As dissimilar as we may appear to be, we are in fact *"one in the bonds of love."*

Nothing affirms this more than the stories being told. What I'm learning again is that it's so important to …

Take time to tell the stories and give God the glory!

Every public presentation and private conversation is dominated by a story!

- ◊ *Stories that confirm what really matters in life and convince us that we are not living in vain.*
- ◊ *Stories that speak of God's goodness and shout of His greatness!*
- ◊ *Stories that encourage us and exalt the name of The Lord our God.*

With the telling of every story, you can almost feel *"faith arise!"*

Each story is received enthusiastically and responded to with exuberant praise to God ... who clearly is the One to make all things possible! Every story leaves its "mark in the heart" and its impact will be passed on from "generation to generation!"

I'm more convinced than ever before that it's so important for us to ...

Take time to tell the stories and give God the glory!

Make it an intentional practice in your family and in your church! Create the opportunity and I promise that good things will happen ... seriously good things!

So, wanna hear a great story?

KEY INSIGHTS

◊ *Do you aspire to live your best life? Embrace a coach, mentor, and advocate.*

◊ *As a leader, what you believe and proclaim is partial. Consistent practice makes it complete and empowers your influence!*

◊ *Quality decision-making positions you to make a quality difference. Provide a lead with proactivity, persistence, and positivity.*

◊ *We lead our lives in a Grand Story. Mini-stories make up the fabric of our lives and those we lead. Tap the power of narrative. Stories move people!*

PRAYER AND AFFIRMATION

Father, I praise you. You call me up in all things! I resolve to attain next-level living and leadership. I welcome and receive the coaches, mentors, and advocates you give me. Holy Spirit, empower me to practice, to live out all that I believe and proclaim. I have the mind of Christ, especially as I am in relationship with key Kingdom people. Give me the insight and courage to make quality decisions. I'm grateful I'm part of your Grand Story. I celebrate and "publish" the mini-stories all around me. Father, I'm so blessed to be connected with you in all of these ways! Amen.

ADVANCING FORWARD

Know that proximity is power ... intentionally relate to coaches, mentors, and advocates. How can you better practice what you believe and proclaim? Make a list and initiate action over the next 60 days. Audit some of the recent decisions you've made. Are you seeing the outcomes you desire? Seek the mind of Christ to level-up your decision-making. Journal some of the beautiful stories you see around you. "Publish" them whenever you can.

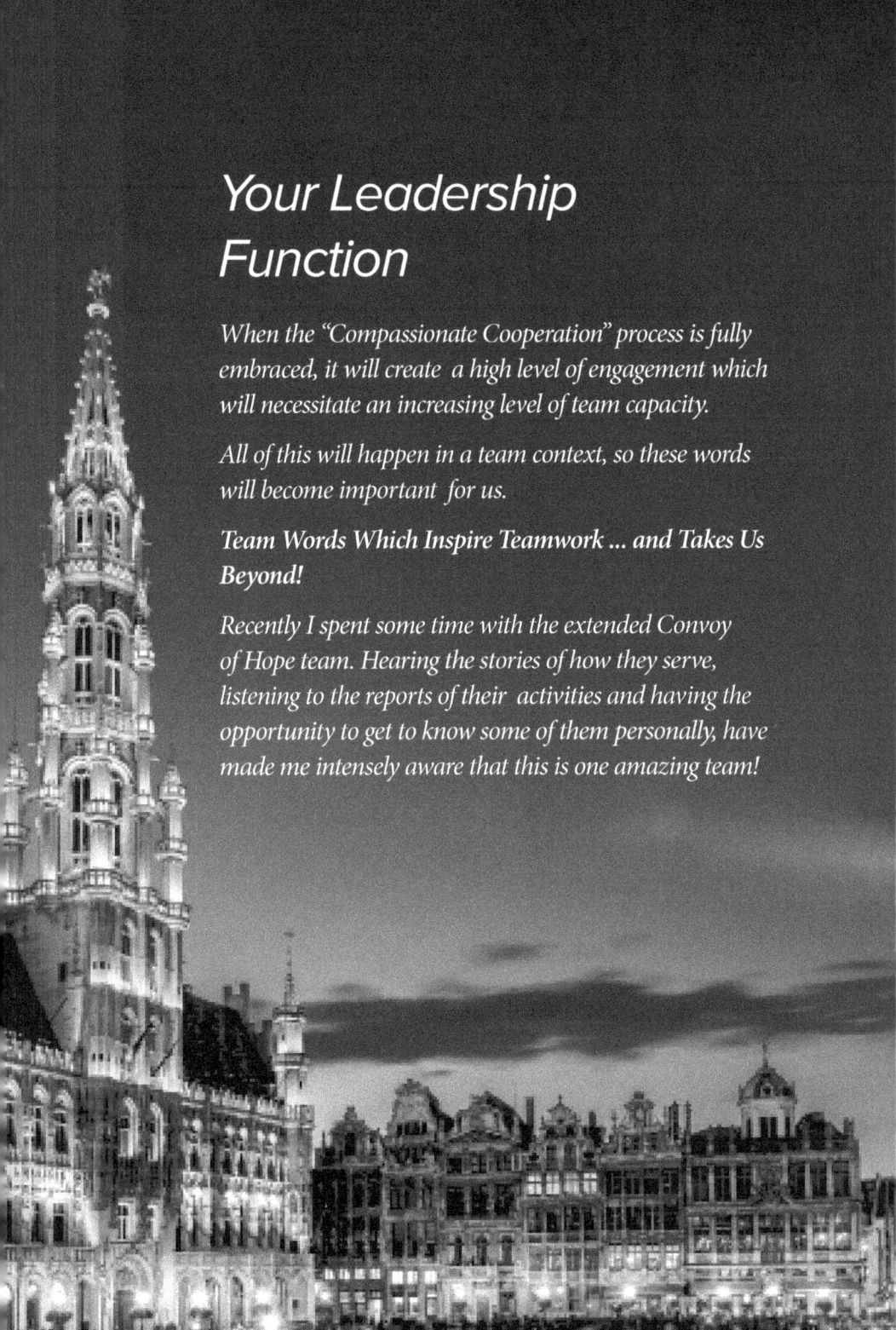

Your Leadership Function

When the "Compassionate Cooperation" process is fully embraced, it will create a high level of engagement which will necessitate an increasing level of team capacity.

All of this will happen in a team context, so these words will become important for us.

Team Words Which Inspire Teamwork ... and Takes Us Beyond!

Recently I spent some time with the extended Convoy of Hope team. Hearing the stories of how they serve, listening to the reports of their activities and having the opportunity to get to know some of them personally, have made me intensely aware that this is one amazing team!

Our Convoy team is a very diverse team and their levels of devotion, desire and dedication are equal across every sector. There was no distinguishable difference ... every person that I encountered was passionately engaged!

What I was immediately aware of is that this kind of commitment is based on covenant. These individuals have made covenant with God, with themselves and with each other ... and that takes them beyond!

As I have considered all I observed this week, what I came away with is this ... what is verbalized among team members matters!

I know we often think about speaking positive words of affirmation which nurture positive attitudes ... and that is a powerful action to initiate.

However, there is something more powerful!

It seems to me that speaking words which promote covenant will take us deeper, and we will begin to think about an alliance being established. This will give us a relational connection which will take us beyond just coming together for a project. It will move us toward serving together with a purpose ... and that position is perfect!

I have always been very intentional about doing my best to inspire teamwork. But now I want to speak words which take my team into covenant.

My sense is this will make all that we do together more than it has ever been before ... and I know this will bring good to all those involved.

This shift is going to serve us well!

Personal Reflection

_____
_____
_____
_____
_____
_____
_____
_____
_____
_____
_____

Afterword

I hope you've enjoyed reading "Compassionate Cooperation" and have found it both provocative and profitable.

My desire for sharing this with you is simple: "All of us have to create processes that enable us to bring people together to accomplish a common goal, and the more diverse the group, the more challenging our task becomes."

The world around us is becoming increasingly divisive, and finding pathways to peace and reconciliation is becoming increasingly difficult. All of us who seek to invest in others and have influence with them will be challenged to find ways to make that happen.

It is into this abyss of aggressiveness that I dare to introduce the potential and possibility of "Compassionate Cooperation."

My sense is that now, more than ever, we need a process that begins by promoting the right heart attitudes and perspectives which will then lead to relational peace and dignity. This will allow covenant and agreement to be established.

My greatest joy has come from seeing the beauty of this "compassionate cooperation" process at work in the lives of those I have been honored to serve. In sharing life together in this way, we have enjoyed seasons of special favor, established deep, personal relationships and experienced His blessing in an unprecedented measure.

My prayer is that these very same things can be true for you!

www.ingramcontent.com/pod-product-compliance
Lightning Source LLC
Chambersburg PA
CBHW061233070526
44584CB00030B/4099